Abundance Success

Think it, feel it, celebrate it, allow your energy to radiate out from you, and let the Universe reflect it back to you.

That's when you know you've hit your M-spot.

The Magical Manifesting spot.

— LINDA WILLOW ROBERTS
The Manifesting Queen

I Love Money Cheque

Fill in the date, your name, and the amount you wish to receive. Cut out your cheque and keep it in a central place where you will see it daily. Any time you see your cheque, feel you've received the money, and appreciate that now you can have or do what you want!

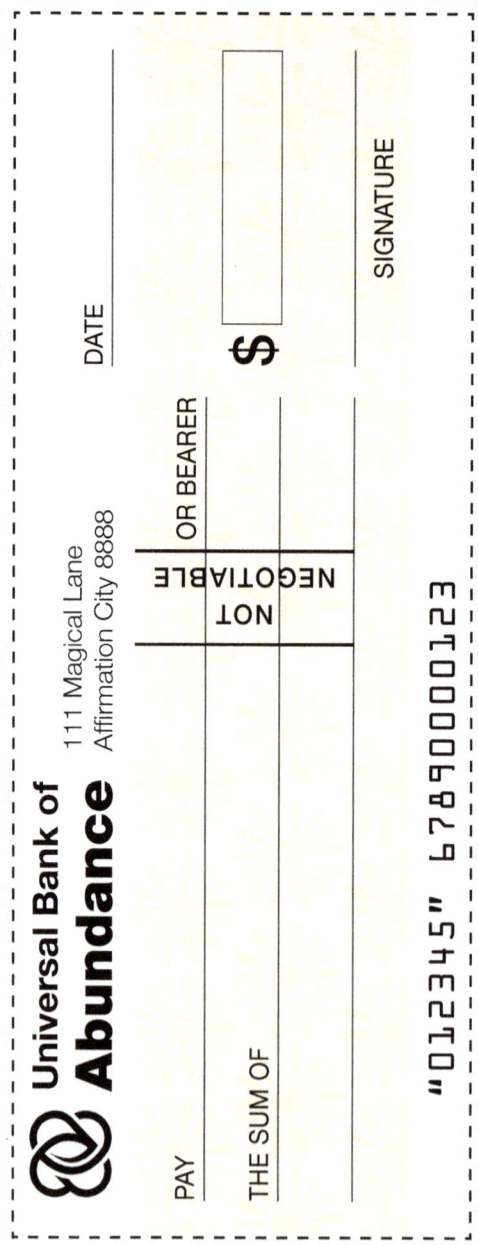

THIS JOURNAL BELONGS TO:

```
┌─────────────────────────────────────────────┐
│                                             │
│                                             │
└─────────────────────────────────────────────┘
```

PLEASE ENJOY THIS JOURNAL AND BE SURE TO VISIT:

www.SpiritualEventsDirectory/Journals

for other beneficial journals and planners

- www.facebook.com/SpiritualEventsDirectory
- www.instagram.com/SpiritualEventsDirectory
- www.twitter.com/SpiritualEvent1

Copyright© 2022 Spiritual Events Directory. All rights reserved. No part of this book may be used or reproduced by any means, graphic, electronic, or mechanical, including photocopying, recording, taping or by any information storage retrieval system without the written permission of the publisher, except in the case of brief quotations embodied in critical articles and reviews.

DISCLAIMER:
The publisher shall not be liable for any physical, psychological, emotional, financial, or commercial damages including, but not limited to, special, incidental, consequential or other damages. Our views and rights are the same: you are responsible for your own choices, actions and results. Seek professional health support if required.

If you have any questions please email: **media@spiritualeventsdirectory.com**

ISBN: 978-0-6450873-8-3

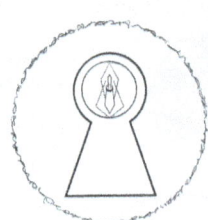

Abundance Code
"You are the key to your abundance. Intention and action are the fundamental tools you provide whilst the Universe envelops you in never-ending possibilities and opportunities. This code initiates the understanding you must rise to meet the Universal Abundance through your physical action and beingness." **This code is part of Soul Light Codes** and Messages Oracle Deck by Annie Caulkett.

Cover artwork by: Annie Caulkett
www.lcstudioau.com \\ fb and insta @lcstudioau

Pubished by: Spiritual Events & Directory

How to Use
THIS JOURNAL

THE SUBCONSCIOUS MIND GENERALLY REQUIRES BETWEEN 22 AND 66 CONSECUTIVE DAYS TO BE REPROGRAMMED.

The *I Love Money Journal* is a 60-day mindset journal to positively help you shift how you think, act, and feel about your money.

It is important that you sign the prosperity declaration and follow the simple money blocks spell.

After this, you are then good to start your daily affirmation journalling from Day 1 to Day 60.

Firstly, you are guided to examine the past and clarify precisely what memories and emotions you're holding onto around money. Where did your money blocks, stories, fears and limiting beliefs come from?

Secondly, the process guides you to focus on the magic of money, your appreciation for it and creating your desires.

Next, is the exciting step of setting your money goals, money strategies, monthly budgeting, savings trackers, saving ideas and more!

Finally, there is the opportunity for you to reflect on your money blocks, stories, fears and limiting beliefs.

I am so excited you said YES to YOU; going on this life-changing journey. Our minds are so powerful and capable of massive transformations. At times, a slight change to rewire your mindset for more abundance and success can make a positive difference in your path forward.

Abundance is everywhere. There is an endless amount of money in circulation, but sometimes our beliefs about money can block us from receiving and allowing all this abundance into our lives.

You can live a prosperous, more abundant life with a few mindset and energetic tweaks. If you consciously choose thoughts that support wealth, money and abundance, your reality can shape to match your thoughts. If you associate wealth with all things good, you can align to the wealth frequency.

I am a single Mum who years ago had a dream to create a new reality for myself and my children, which does require money and at the time I had the bare minimum.

I began a daily regime of using the affirmations I share with you in the *I Love Money Journal,* as well as the money, prompts and budget worksheets. These have firmly helped me to develop long-lasting change.

Ten years ago, I manifested the *Spiritual Events Directory* and since have grown its wealth to a level that I can financially support me and my children, as well as creating a network of people that is focused on spiritual/personal development and wellbeing.

Imagine what you can create for yourself, your family and the world! Let's get started.

Sarah Jayd

Contents

Prosperity Declaration	07
Spell To Remove Money Blocks	08
My Feelings About Money	10
My Fears About Money	15
My Limiting Beliefs	20
An Attitude of Gratitude	23
My Money Actions	24
My Money Declaration	25
Create Magic	26
I Love Money	27
Imagine Your Desire, Create Your Desire	28
Abundance Affirmations	30
Negatives To Positives	31
Positive Daily Affirmations	32
Daily Affirmations	33
My Money Goals	93
My Money Strategy	97
Monthly Intentions	100
Monthly Review	103
Monthly Budgeting	105
Savings Trackers	109
Reducing Debt	113
My Monthly Bills	115
My Yearly Bills	116
Subscription Services	117
My Money Saving Ideas	119
Possessions I Can Sell	122
Online Sales Listings	122
Reflection – My Feelings About Money	123
Reflection – My Fears About Money	127
Celebrating You	131

Prosperity DECLARATION

SAY A FEW TIMES A WEEK:

Today and every day, I choose to have a powerful Millionaire Mindset and create an amazing life.

I am one with my Creator, giving and receiving prosperity in a continuous flow of love and abundance.

I only align with experiences and feelings that serve my highest vibration.

I choose to attract wealth and make a difference in the world.

The Divine light flows through me, filling every cell of my being with prosperity and abundance.

I am brave, strong and confident.

I am ready to create miracles in my life.

I choose to grow and evolve; it is safe for me to be abundant.

I am always protected by the Universe.

I am powerful, authentic, magical and unique.

I allow all this and more by divine right and for the highest good of all concerned.

And so, it is!

Date: _____

Sign: _____

Spell
TO REMOVE MONEY BLOCKS

Harness the power of the moon and all the planetary influences. This spell is best done on a waning moon.
Visit: http://www.alissandramoon.com for moon cycles.

You will need a piece of paper with "MONEY BLOCKS" written across it.

Before beginning the spell, do the following: (If you do not know how, just take some deep breaths and breathe in peace, breathe out anything that does not serve you. Imagine that you are encapsulated in a big crystal-like bubble that allows only the right energies inside. You can then move on to the spell).

Centre and Ground.
Clear the Space.
Cast your circle and ask the elemental guardians to join you and open the gates to their realm.
E.g.: "Name... Guardian of AIR, I ask that you aid me in my rite. Please open the gate to the realm of air, so the element of air may be present here, enhancing my magick."

Say something in your own words to honour the moon. She is waning between Full and Dark phase.

State your intent:
"I stand here this night (day) in sacred space and command that all bonds, contracts, curses and vows of lack and poverty be undone NOW!" (Click fingers or clap hands.)

"All energetic, psychic, spiritual, mental and emotional blockages that are in any way preventing me from receiving and maintaining financial abundance
I hereby banish!

Be gone NOW!
All roads are open to receive that which is good.
Money is good.
Money is safe.
Money is love.

Money loves me
And I love money!
It is safe to have money.
I always have money,
All that I need and plenty to spare,
Money to spend and money to share.
Money is good!
Money is good!
Money is good!"

Now as you gradually raise the paper up in front of you, chant this verse.
With each round, raise the intensity and energy, imagining the limiting beliefs, energies, and any blocks coming out of you and your energy field, flying away and dissolving.

"Money blocks, it's time to go!
As the moon is waning slow,
Transform all negativity,
To abundance and prosperity!"

When the paper is in front of your face and the energy reaches its peak,
Violently rip it in half!
You can rip it right up into little pieces or scrunch it up then burn it or bury it asking the fire or earth to transform your money blocks into prosperity.

Sit and focus on how life will be when you have no money worries, and lots of money.
Imagine it like its already happened.
In reverse order, thank and farewell your deity, the elements and guardians,
Open your circle.
Ground.

FORGET ABOUT THE SPELL and TRUST THAT IT WORKED.
THERE IS NO OTHER OPTION!!

ALISSANDRA MOON
Raven Moon Academy of Magick
www.alissandramoon.com

My Feelings
ABOUT MONEY

What was I taught about money growing up?

_____
_____
_____
_____
_____
_____
_____
_____
_____
_____
_____
_____
_____
_____
_____
_____
_____
_____
_____
_____

What does money mean to me?

How do I feel when spending money on bills, education, food, travel, entertainment and more?

___
___
___
___
___
___
___
___
___
___
___
___
___
___
___
___
___
___
___
___
___

What have I learnt about money in the last five years?

_____
_____
_____
_____
_____
_____
_____
_____
_____
_____
_____
_____
_____
_____
_____
_____
_____
_____
_____
_____
_____
_____
_____

How do I feel when receiving money?

My Fears
ABOUT MONEY

When it comes to money, what stresses me out?

_____
_____
_____
_____
_____
_____
_____
_____
_____
_____
_____
_____
_____
_____
_____
_____
_____
_____
_____
_____

What fears do I have about running out of money tomorrow?

Do I have one or more skills that could make me money, but I have been afraid to use it?

_____
_____
_____
_____
_____
_____
_____
_____
_____
_____
_____
_____
_____
_____
_____
_____
_____
_____
_____
_____
_____
_____
_____

What is my biggest financial fear?

Do I feel worthy of earning more money? Why/Why not?

My Limiting BELIEFS

When it comes to working on your money mindset, it is important to look inside yourself. The negative beliefs you have about yourself can hold you back. They can limit your ability to grow, move forward, earn more or save more. Writing these beliefs down may feel challenging, however, this is a process that can help free up those beliefs.

I believe… _____

_____

_____

_____

_____

_____

_____

I believe… _____

_____

_____

_____

_____

_____

_____

I believe...

I believe...

I believe... _____
_____
_____
_____
_____
_____
_____
_____
_____

I believe... _____
_____
_____
_____
_____
_____
_____
_____
_____

An Attitude
OF GRATITUDE

Write down at least 22 things you are grateful for right now.

1. _____
2. _____
3. _____
4. _____
5. _____
6. _____
7. _____
8. _____
9. _____
10. _____
11. _____
12. _____
13. _____
14. _____
15. _____
16. _____
17. _____
18. _____
19. _____
20. _____
21. _____
22. _____

My Money
ACTIONS

Write down the actions you are committed to take in order to earn more money and/or cut down your expenses:

ACTIONS TO EARN	ACTIONS TO CUT DOWN

My Money
DECLARATION

Take the limiting beliefs from the previous pages and reword them until they say the complete opposite to what you originally wrote down. Write these new statements on this page as one long, positive, statement. This is your new Money Declaration.

_____
_____
_____
_____
_____
_____
_____
_____
_____
_____
_____
_____
_____
_____
_____
_____

Create Magic

Take a moment to write down what your ideal day would look like. What would you be doing? How would you be feeling? How would your life be different?

_____
_____
_____
_____
_____
_____
_____
_____
_____
_____
_____
_____
_____
_____
_____
_____
_____
_____
_____
_____

I Love Money

Write down at least 22 times – "I love money and money loves me."

1. _____
2. _____
3. _____
4. _____
5. _____
6. _____
7. _____
8. _____
9. _____
10. _____
11. _____
12. _____
13. _____
14. _____
15. _____
16. _____
17. _____
18. _____
19. _____
20. _____
21. _____
22. _____

Imagine Your Desire
CREATE YOUR DESIRE

Write down what it is you want to attract into your life – be specific. Example, rather than just say, a new house, describe what the house looks like inside and out, and how you would feel living in it.

_____
_____
_____
_____
_____
_____
_____
_____
_____
_____
_____
_____
_____
_____
_____
_____

Take a photo and place it here, or cut out a picture in a magazine that represents what you want to attract into your life.

Abundance
AFFIRMATIONS

Write down at least 22 Abundance Affirmations, i.e. "I am worthy of what I desire, I have everything I need to be successful."

1. _____
2. _____
3. _____
4. _____
5. _____
6. _____
7. _____
8. _____
9. _____
10. _____
11. _____
12. _____
13. _____
14. _____
15. _____
16. _____
17. _____
18. _____
19. _____
20. _____
21. _____
22. _____

Negatives TO POSITIVES

Phrasing your negative thoughts and feelings about money into positive alternatives. Once you've done this, every time you find yourself slipping into negative thinking, catch yourself and switch it to something positive.

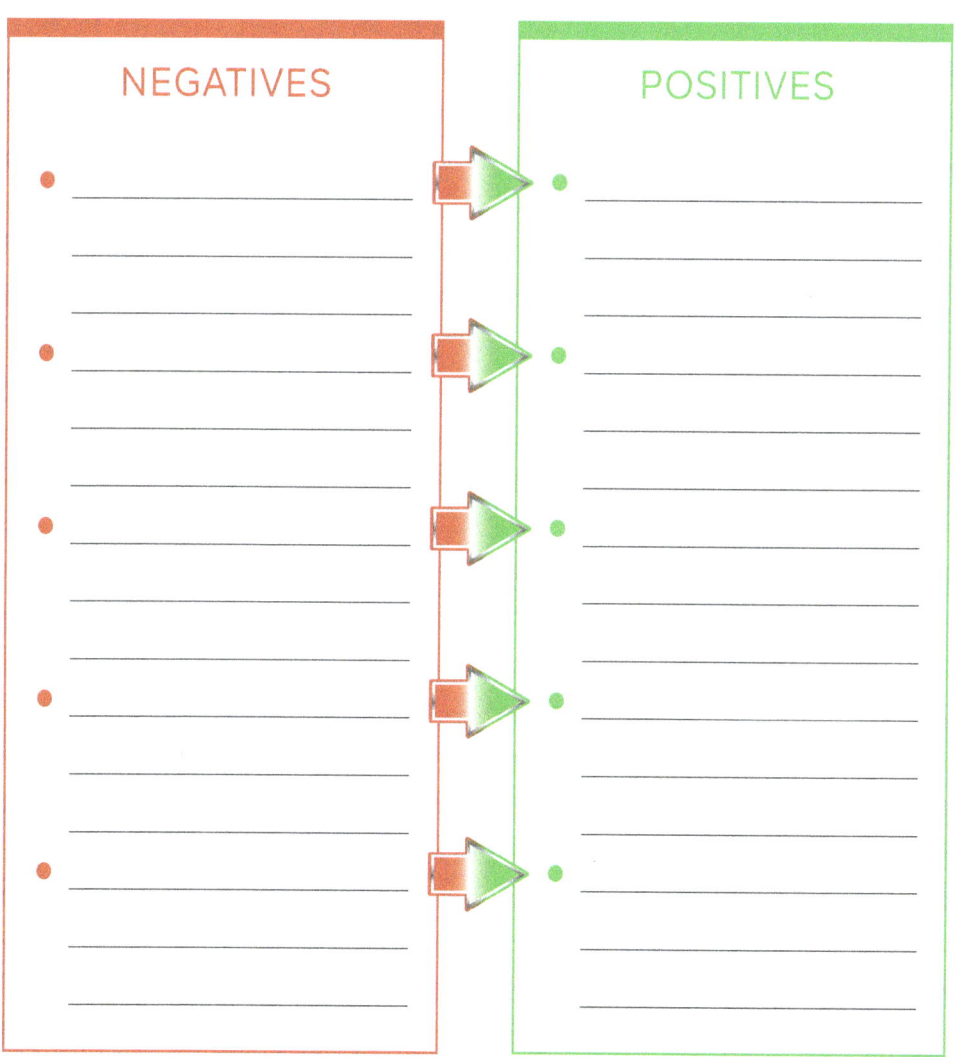

Positive DAILY AFFIRMATIONS

Now, take all your positives from the previous page, and turn them into positive affirmations that you can repeat to yourself daily. The stronger they are, and the more you repeat them, the more of an impact they will have on your mindset.

- I am... _____
  I have... _____
  I can... _____

- I am... _____
  I have... _____
  I can... _____

- I am... _____
  I have... _____
  I can... _____

- I am... _____
  I have... _____
  I can... _____

- I am... _____
  I have... _____
  I can... _____

DAY 1:

Daily Affirmations

Use these pages to write your affirmations daily for the next 60 days.

Date: _____

_____
_____
_____
_____
_____
_____
_____
_____
_____
_____
_____
_____
_____
_____
_____
_____
_____

"I am worthy of what I desire."

DAY 2:

Date: _____

"I attract money to me easily and effortlessly."

DAY 3:

Date: _____

_____
_____
_____
_____
_____
_____
_____
_____
_____
_____
_____
_____
_____
_____
_____
_____
_____
_____
_____

"I have access to what I need to be successful."

DAY 4:

Date: _____

"I am worthy of the wealth I desire."

DAY 5:

Date: _____

"I am grateful for the positive things in my life."

DAY 6:

Date: _____

"I change the world with my money."

DAY 7:

Date: _____

"I am open to limitless possibilities."

DAY 8:

Date: _____

"I am generous with my money."

DAY 9:

Date: _____

___

"I achieve whatever I set my mind to."

DAY 10:

Date: _____

_____
_____
_____
_____
_____
_____
_____
_____
_____
_____
_____
_____
_____
_____
_____
_____
_____

"I believe there is enough money for everyone."

DAY 11:

Date: _____

"I am smart, capable and talented."

DAY 12:

Date: _____

_____
_____
_____
_____
_____
_____
_____
_____
_____
_____
_____
_____
_____
_____
_____
_____
_____
_____
_____

"I love money because money loves me."

DAY 13:

Date: _____

"I believe in myself."

DAY 14:

Date: _____

"I am ready to share my gifts with the world."

DAY 15:

Date: _____

_____
_____
_____
_____
_____
_____
_____
_____
_____
_____
_____
_____
_____
_____
_____
_____
_____
_____
_____
_____
_____
_____
_____
_____

"I am grateful for money."

DAY 16:

Date: _____

"I make money easily."

DAY 17:

Date: _____

"I surrender to the wisdom of the Universe."

DAY 18:

Date: _____

"I am a money magnet."

DAY 19:

Date: _____

_____
_____
_____
_____
_____
_____
_____
_____
_____
_____
_____
_____
_____
_____
_____
_____
_____
_____
_____
_____
_____
_____

"I am my best source of motivation."

DAY 20:

Date: _____

"I always have enough money."

DAY 21:

Date: _____

"I am creative and open to new solutions."

DAY 22:

Date: _____

"I choose to embrace the mystery of life."

DAY 23:

Date: _____

"I am choosing faith over fear."

DAY 24:

Date: _____

" I allow everything to be as it is. "

DAY 25:

Date: _____

"I attract miracles into my life."

DAY 26:

Date: _____

"I am open to receiving unexpected opportunities."

DAY 27:

Date: _____

"I am aligned with my purpose."

DAY 28:

Date: _____

_____
_____
_____
_____
_____
_____
_____
_____
_____
_____
_____
_____
_____
_____
_____
_____
_____
_____

"I am worthy of positive changes in my life."

DAY 29:

Date: _____

"I am grateful for the abundance that I have and the abundance that's on its way."

DAY 30:

Date: _____

_____
_____
_____
_____
_____
_____
_____
_____
_____
_____
_____
_____
_____
_____
_____
_____
_____
_____

"I am capable of achieving greatness."

DAY 31:

Date: _____

"I attract money quickly and easily."

DAY 32:

Date: _____

"Money is energy and energy is limitless."

DAY 33:

Date: _____

"Success is always flowing to me."

DAY 34:

Date: _____

"I am a magnet for million-dollar ideas."

DAY 35:

Date: _____

_____
_____
_____
_____
_____
_____
_____
_____
_____
_____
_____
_____
_____
_____
_____
_____
_____
_____
_____
_____
_____

"I am ready for abundance."

DAY 36:

Date: _____

"I am wealthy, happy and healthy."

DAY 37:

Date: _____

"I am prosperous and attract
a prosperous tribe."

DAY 38:

Date: _____

"Having plenty of money is my natural state of being."

DAY 39:

Date: _____

"Money can't stay away from me."

DAY 40:

Date: _____

_____
_____
_____
_____
_____
_____
_____
_____
_____
_____
_____
_____
_____
_____
_____
_____
_____
_____

"I am a bountiful millionaire."

DAY 41:

Date: _____

"My relationship with money is healthy."

DAY 42:

Date: _____

_____
_____
_____
_____
_____
_____
_____
_____
_____
_____
_____
_____
_____
_____
_____
_____
_____

"I always manifest the financial resources I need in the time frame I need it."

DAY 43:

Date: _____

_____
_____
_____
_____
_____
_____
_____
_____
_____
_____
_____
_____
_____
_____
_____
_____
_____
_____
_____
_____
_____

"I am financially responsible."

DAY 44:

Date: _____

"My bank account is always full."

DAY 45:

Date: _____

"Every day I am becoming richer and richer."

DAY 46:

Date: _____

"I am a frequency match for wealth and prosperity."

DAY 47:

Date: _____

"I have a wealth mindset."

DAY 48:

Date: _____

_____
_____
_____
_____
_____
_____
_____
_____
_____
_____
_____
_____
_____
_____
_____
_____

"I am grateful for everything I receive."

DAY 49:

Date: _____

"My wealth shines from within me."

DAY 50:

Date: _____

"I only think thoughts of wealth and abundance."

DAY 51:

Date: _____

"I am a wealthy entrepreneur living life on my terms."

DAY 52:

Date: _____

_____
_____
_____
_____
_____
_____
_____
_____
_____
_____
_____
_____
_____
_____
_____
_____

"The faith I have in myself allows me to be successful."

DAY 53:

Date: _____

"I have the discipline to become rich."

DAY 54:

Date: _____

"I am capable to overcome any money obstacles that stand in my way."

DAY 55:

Date: _____

"I control money.
Money does not control me."

DAY 56:

Date: _____

_____
_____
_____
_____
_____
_____
_____
_____
_____
_____
_____
_____
_____
_____
_____
_____
_____
_____

"I trust that more money is coming to me."

DAY 57:

Date: _____

___

"It's easy to make money."

DAY 58:

Date: _____

"I know that money is freedom."

DAY 59:

Date: _____

_____
_____
_____
_____
_____
_____
_____
_____
_____
_____
_____
_____
_____
_____
_____
_____
_____
_____
_____

"I breathe in abundance and breathe out scarcity."

DAY 60:

Date: _____

"I welcome an unlimited source of income into my life."

My Money
GOALS

Goal #1:

Goal #2:

Goal #3:

Goal #4:

Goal #5:

Goal #6:

"I am the master of my wealth."

Goal #7:

Goal #8:

Goal #9:

"I breathe in abundance."

Goal #10:

MINDMAP

"My income is always higher than my expenses."

My Money STRATEGY

Write down the knowledge areas, skills, trainings, or books to read so that you can learn to achieve your money goals:

"I am successful with money."

"I am worthy of making more money."

Monthly INTENTIONS

Intention #1:

What is my intention for this month?

_____
_____
_____
_____
_____
_____
_____

How will I do this?

_____
_____
_____
_____
_____
_____
_____
_____

Intention #2:

What is my intention for this month?

_____
_____
_____
_____
_____
_____
_____
_____

How will I do this?

_____
_____
_____
_____
_____
_____
_____
_____

Intention #3:

What is my intention for this month?

_____
_____
_____
_____
_____
_____
_____

How will I do this?

_____
_____
_____
_____
_____
_____
_____

Monthly
REVIEW

Month of: _____

Achieved?

Y / N

MY MONEY GOALS

_____
_____
_____
_____

☐ ☐
☐ ☐
☐ ☐
☐ ☐

MY BALANCES

Account	Start $	$ In	$ Out	End $
Note:			Total End $	

How does the above align with my budget?

I Love Money Journal

What worked?	What went wrong?

What I learned?	What to improve?

Does the above align with my financial values?

Monthly BUDGETING

Month of: _____

HOUSEHOLD

Expense	Budget	Actual
M/Rent		
Insurance		
Electric		
Water		
Phone		
TV/Internet		
Subtotal		

FOOD

Expense	Budget	Actual
Groceries		
Dining Out		
Subtotal		

HEALTH

Expense	Budget	Actual
Insurance		
Prescription		
Subtotal		

SCHOOL

Expense	Budget	Actual
Personal		
Student		
Credit		
Subtotal		

PERSONAL

Expense	Budget	Actual
Clothing		
Self-Care		
Exercise		
Subtotal		

ENTERTAINMENT

Expense	Budget	Actual
Events		
Hobbies		
Subtotal		

TRANSPORT

Expense	Budget	Actual
Insurance		
Repairs		
Registration		
Fuel		
Subtotal		

OTHER

Expense	Budget	Actual
Subtotal		

Total Budgeted	Total Actual	Difference

NOTES

Monthly BUDGETING

Month of: _____

HOUSEHOLD

Expense	Budget	Actual
M/Rent		
Insurance		
Electric		
Water		
Phone		
TV/Internet		
Subtotal		

FOOD

Expense	Budget	Actual
Groceries		
Dining Out		
Subtotal		

HEALTH

Expense	Budget	Actual
Insurance		
Prescription		
Subtotal		

SCHOOL

Expense	Budget	Actual
Personal		
Student		
Credit		
Subtotal		

PERSONAL

Expense	Budget	Actual
Clothing		
Self-Care		
Exercise		
Subtotal		

ENTERTAINMENT

Expense	Budget	Actual
Events		
Hobbies		
Subtotal		

TRANSPORT

Expense	Budget	Actual
Insurance		
Repairs		
Registration		
Fuel		
Subtotal		

OTHER

Expense	Budget	Actual
Subtotal		

Total Budgeted	Total Actual	Difference

NOTES

Savings TRACKERS

Saving For	$ Amount	By

Date	Deposit	New Total

WAYS TO EARN/SAVE FOR THIS

Saving For	$ Amount	By

Date	Deposit	New Total

WAYS TO EARN/SAVE FOR THIS

"I am in control of my spending."

Saving For	$ Amount	By

Date	Deposit	New Total

WAYS TO EARN/SAVE FOR THIS

"Every dollar saved puts me closer to financial freedom."

Saving For	$ Amount	By

Date	Deposit	New Total

WAYS TO EARN/SAVE FOR THIS

"I am a successful money saver."

Reducing DEBT

I Owe Money To	$ Debt	I Will Pay It By

Date	$ Paid	New Balance

Minimum Payment

Interest Rate

PAYING THIS WILL MEAN:

I Owe Money To	$ Debt	I Will Pay It By

Date	$ Paid	New Balance

Minimum Payment

Interest Rate

PAYING THIS WILL MEAN:

"My debt doesn't control me; I manage it."

My Monthly
BILLS

Bill Name	Due Date	$ Owed	Month Paid J F M A M J J A S O N D
			☐☐☐☐☐☐☐☐☐☐☐☐
			☐☐☐☐☐☐☐☐☐☐☐☐
			☐☐☐☐☐☐☐☐☐☐☐☐
			☐☐☐☐☐☐☐☐☐☐☐☐
			☐☐☐☐☐☐☐☐☐☐☐☐
			☐☐☐☐☐☐☐☐☐☐☐☐
			☐☐☐☐☐☐☐☐☐☐☐☐
			☐☐☐☐☐☐☐☐☐☐☐☐
			☐☐☐☐☐☐☐☐☐☐☐☐
			☐☐☐☐☐☐☐☐☐☐☐☐
			☐☐☐☐☐☐☐☐☐☐☐☐
			☐☐☐☐☐☐☐☐☐☐☐☐
			☐☐☐☐☐☐☐☐☐☐☐☐
			☐☐☐☐☐☐☐☐☐☐☐☐
			☐☐☐☐☐☐☐☐☐☐☐☐

"I am grateful that I get to pay these bills."

My Yearly BILLS

Bill Name	Due Date	$ Owed	Month Paid J F M A M J J A S O N D
			☐☐☐☐☐☐☐☐☐☐☐☐
			☐☐☐☐☐☐☐☐☐☐☐☐
			☐☐☐☐☐☐☐☐☐☐☐☐
			☐☐☐☐☐☐☐☐☐☐☐☐
			☐☐☐☐☐☐☐☐☐☐☐☐
			☐☐☐☐☐☐☐☐☐☐☐☐
			☐☐☐☐☐☐☐☐☐☐☐☐
			☐☐☐☐☐☐☐☐☐☐☐☐
			☐☐☐☐☐☐☐☐☐☐☐☐
			☐☐☐☐☐☐☐☐☐☐☐☐
			☐☐☐☐☐☐☐☐☐☐☐☐
			☐☐☐☐☐☐☐☐☐☐☐☐
			☐☐☐☐☐☐☐☐☐☐☐☐
			☐☐☐☐☐☐☐☐☐☐☐☐
			☐☐☐☐☐☐☐☐☐☐☐☐

"I am grateful that I get to pay these bills."

Subscription
SERVICES

Name:					
Type	Started	Cost	Expires	Length	Payment Type

Name:					
Type	Started	Cost	Expires	Length	Payment Type

Name:					
Type	Started	Cost	Expires	Length	Payment Type

Name:					
Type	Started	Cost	Expires	Length	Payment Type

Name:					
Type	Started	Cost	Expires	Length	Payment Type

Name:					
Type	Started	Cost	Expires	Length	Payment Type

Name:					
Type	Started	Cost	Expires	Length	Payment Type

Name:					
Type	Started	Cost	Expires	Length	Payment Type

Name:					
Type	Started	Cost	Expires	Length	Payment Type

Name:					
Type	Started	Cost	Expires	Length	Payment Type

Name:					
Type	Started	Cost	Expires	Length	Payment Type

Name:					
Type	Started	Cost	Expires	Length	Payment Type

Name:					
Type	Started	Cost	Expires	Length	Payment Type

Name:					
Type	Started	Cost	Expires	Length	Payment Type

"I manifest enough income to pay for the lifestyle I want."

My Money
SAVING IDEAS

1.

2.

3.

4.

5.

6.

I Love Money Journal

Take the money saving ideas you jotted down in the stars on the previous page and write a mini "I will" plan on this page.

Idea #1: I will…

Idea #2: I will…

Idea #3: I will…

Idea #4:   I will...

Idea #5:   I will...

Idea #6:   I will...

"I am grateful for my money making ideas."

Possessions
I CAN SELL

Item	Am I Sure?	Value	Where?

Online
SALES LISTINGS

Item	Price	Website	Until	Sold?	Sent?
				☐	☐
				☐	☐
				☐	☐
				☐	☐
				☐	☐
				☐	☐

Reflection
MY FEELINGS ABOUT MONEY

Use these pages to reflect on the questions you answered at the start of this journal. Have your answers changed?

How have I built a more loving relationship with money?

_____
_____
_____
_____
_____
_____
_____
_____
_____
_____
_____
_____
_____
_____
_____
_____
_____
_____

Reflection
MY FEARS ABOUT MONEY

Use these pages to reflect on the questions you answered at the start of this journal. Have your answers changed?

How do I now feel safer about my relationship with money?

_____
_____
_____
_____
_____
_____
_____
_____
_____
_____
_____
_____
_____
_____
_____
_____
_____

Celebrating You

The 60-day adventure is a wonderful transformational journey. By the end of the 60 days celebrate you and the miracles you've seen along the way and those still to come! Please share your 60-day realisations and results with us on Facebook or Instagram – @SpiritualEventsDirectory #SpiritualEventsDirectory

Let's finish off with a Simple Money Spell to cement the journey.

YOU WILL NEED:
1 green, gold or white candle
1 pin or sharp object for engraving the candle
A few drops of oil – Cooking oil is fine
Dried or fresh Basil, chopped finely
Candle holder and lighter

New Moon or anytime the Moon is waxing (growing to full but BEFORE it is full).
Sit and take some deep breaths, clearing your mind and exhaling any unhelpful energies.
Imagine a crystalline bubble forming around you and purifying all the energies inside.
Take the pin and carve your name into the candle.
Now carve as many dollar signs as you feel is right. Whilst you do it, imagine yourself as already having plenty of money.
Anoint/rub the candle with oil starting at each end and rubbing INWARDS, towards the centre.
Continue the visualisation as you do this. Remember that you need to not only picture yourself having money, but really FEEL it.
Roll the candle in basil.
Place the candle in a holder on your altar and light it.

CHANT:
"By the power of the moon I say
Money flows to me each day.
Good fortune comes without delay!
Abundant me, in every way!"

Continue to chant and raise the energy. You can dance and clap and drum to add to the energy raising.
When you feel that you have built up enough energy, throw your arms up in the air and with absolute conviction, state "IT IS DONE!"
Now just sit and watch the candle for a while.
If it is safe to do so, let it burn down.
Place what is left of the candle somewhere safe for at least one full moon cycle. (In the south-east area of your home preferably, but its not imperative.)
Now just trust that it has worked. DO NOT talk about it, share photos, dwell, worry or think about it.
Just know that it is done and LET IT GO! Otherwise, you will pull back and confuse the energy of the spell.

www.alissandramoon.com

PARTNERSHIP OPPORTUNITY

Spiritual Events Directory (SED) specialises in showcasing conscious leaders to become recognised authorities and leading experts through a variety of mediums:

The Spirituality Show, Magazine publication, Social Media, Online Directory, and Book/Journal publishing.

SED provides the opportunity for you to tap into your potential as a creative whilst reaching a network of over 150,000 members.

You are always in control while benefiting from our expert guidance as your idea is transformed into reality.

www.SpiritualEventsDirectory.com